THE U.S. MARINES
SPECIAL OPERATIONS REGIMENT

The Missions

by Craig Sodaro

Consultant
James C. Bradford
Professor of History
Texas A&M

CAPSTONE PRESS
a capstone imprint

Velocity is published by Capstone Press,
1710 Roe Crest Drive, North Mankato, Minnesota 56003.
www.capstonepub.com

Library of Congress Cataloging-in-Publication Data
Sodaro, Craig.
The U.S. Marines Special Operations Regiment : the missions / by Craig Sodaro.
p. cm.—(Velocity. American special ops.)
Includes bibliographical references and index.
Summary: "Describes the U.S. Marines Special Operations Regiment, including the group's
history, weapons, gear, and missions"—Provided by publisher.
Audience: Grades 4-6.
ISBN 978-1-4296-8658-7 (library binding)
ISBN 978-1-62065-356-2 (ebook pdf)
1. United States. Marine Special Operations Command   Juvenile literature. 2. Special
operations (Military science)—Juvenile literature. I. Title. II. Title: US Marines Special
Operations Regiment.
VE23.S59 2013
359.9'6—dc23   2012003133

Editorial Credits
Jennifer Besel, editor; Veronica Correia, designer; Laura Manthe,
production specialist

Photo Credits
Corbis: Bettmann, 19, Hulton-Deutsch Collection, 19 (inset), Philip Cheung, 43 (bottom),
Science Faction/Ed Darack, 10; DoD photo, 12 (top), John Yoder, 31 (bottom), Lance Cpl.
Stephen C. Benson, 1, 44, Master Sgt. Jeremiah Erickson, USAF, 12 (bottom), Staff Sgt.
Matthew O. Holly, 45 (top), Staff Sgt. Rasheen Douglas, 34-35; Newscom: akg-Images, 18,
Publmages, 16; Shutterstock: Antenna International, 18 (map), AridOcean, 8-9 (map),
Digital Storm, 23, Peter Kim, 31 (top), Pjasha, 36 (map); U.S. Air Force photo by Tech. Sgt.
Sean M. Worrell, 35 (middle); U.S. Marine Corps photo, 14-15, 20 (both), 21, 27 (inset), 31
(middle), 33 (top), 43 (top), Cpl. Christopher R. Rye, 35 (top), Cpl. Kyle McNally, 7 (inset), 13
(top), 24, 39, cover, Cpl. Michael A. Bianco, 45 (bottom), Cpl. Richard Blumenstein, 32, Lance
Cpl. Stephen Benson, 13 (bottom), Lance Cpl. Thomas W. Provost, 25, 26 (inset), 40-41
(background), Sgt. Brain Kester, 28, 29, 36-37, 35 (bottom), Sgt. Edmund L. Hatch, 4-5, Sgt.
Mark Fayloga, 45 (middle), Sgt. Steven King, 6 Staff Sgt. Luis P. Valdespino Jr., 42 (bottom),
Staff Sgt. Rasheen Douglas, 42 (top); U.S. Navy photo by MC1 Troy Latham, 9 (inset),
MC3 Daisy Abonza, 11 (inset), MCSN Tim Godbee, 33 (bottom), PHAN John P. Curtis, 30
(bottom); Wikimedia: CIA, 17, Kroush, 30 (middle), Mike Searson, 30 (top), Marcus Aurelius
Antoninus, 31 (middle)

Artistic Effects
Shutterstock

Printed in the United States of America in Stevens Point, Wisconsin.

032012   006678WZF12

TABLE OF CONTENTS

FIERCE
FIGHTERS

Just before dawn, soldiers silently jump into a compound. They plant an explosive by the door and light the fuse. In minutes a terrorist hideout is destroyed.

The mission runs just like the men planned. This isn't the first time these soldiers have faced danger. They do it every day.

THEY'RE THE SOLDIERS OF THE U.S. MARINES SPECIAL OPERATIONS REGIMENT.

compound—a grouping of separate homes often enclosed by a fence or wall

terrorist—a person who uses violence to kill or injure to make people and governments afraid

All Marines are well-trained to handle most combat situations. At times, however, regular warfare can't get the job done. That's where the Marines Special Operations Regiment comes in. Members of this team are trained to handle unusual combat situations.

Marines of the Special Operations Regiment are highly trained to work with foreign armies, defeat terrorists, and gather information. The Marine Special Operations Command (MARSOC) gives orders to the Regiment. For this reason the skilled and dedicated Marine special ops soldiers are known as MARSOC Marines.

Chapter 1

TRAINED AND READY

MARSOC Marines are trained to handle many different kinds of missions. They do whatever it takes to keep the United States safe.

Fact

Only men can be MARSOC Marines. By law, women cannot be assigned to combat positions.

DIRECT ACTION

Direct action missions call for secrecy, quick force, and fast exits. These missions put soldiers directly in the line of fire.

MARSOC Marines are trained in several direct action fighting methods, including:

close-quarters combat

hand-to-hand combat

use of explosives

firing shoulder-launched missiles and grenades

MARSOC Marines also become experts on foreign weapons. They learn how far the weapons fire and how many rounds they shoot. They also race to disassemble and assemble the weapons to become familiar with exactly how they work. MARSOC soldiers need this information so they can use foreign weapons on direct action missions if necessary.

FOREIGN INTERNAL DEFENSE

Many countries don't have armies skilled enough to stop an attack. MARSOC soldiers train foreign armies to become more skillful fighters. This type of mission is called foreign internal defense.

Foreign internal defense has proved successful in parts of Iraq. In 2008 Anbar Province was firmly held by the terrorist group al-Qaida. Marines began patrolling the area day and night. They destroyed enemy hideouts and trained the local police. They also helped sharpen the Iraqi army's fighting skills. The Iraqis and the Marines were then able to push al-Qaida out of the area.

MARSOC Trainings around the World

Dominican Republic

Mauritania

Senegal

Mali

Niger

Chad

Colombia

Peru

Bolivia

Understanding Others

Special operations Marines need to understand the culture of the country they operate in. A big part of the culture is a country's language. Many MARSOC Marines learn to speak another language. Marines take a pre-test to see how easily they'll learn another language. Their score determines what language they'll be taught. Classes run six hours a day, five days a week. And there's nightly homework.

Iraq

Israel

Afghanistan

Philippines

SPECIAL RECONNAISSANCE

Before any direct action can take place, MARSOC Marines need to know what, where, and who the target is. MARSOC soldiers are trained in several reconnaissance techniques.

ADVANCED PATROLLING

Soldiers learn how to observe an area to learn about any obstacles.

RADIO COMMUNICATIONS

The men use radios that only send and receive calls from radios equipped with the same software.

MAPPING INFORMATION

MARSOC soldiers make maps that pinpoint civilian areas. This information is important so attack plans can be made that keep civilians out of harm's way.

NAVIGATION

MARSOC Marines are experts at finding their way to enemy hideouts and other hidden locations.

SURVEILLANCE

MARSOC soldiers are trained to follow and watch enemy targets.

reconnaissance—a mission to gather information about an enemy
civilian—a person who is not in the military

Most special reconnaissance requires real people to go into enemy territory. But sometimes MARSOC can use technology instead. They use unmanned aircraft such as the Wasp III to track a target.

The Wasp III can be collapsed to fit in a small case. It weighs about 14 pounds (6 kilograms).

High-definition cameras on the Wasp take pictures behind enemy lines.

MARSOC soldiers hand-launch the Wasp from a safe place. Then it travels into enemy territory.

Fact

Each WASP III costs about $49,000.

UNCONVENTIONAL WARFARE

When people think of war, they most often think of huge armies facing one another. This situation is conventional warfare. MARSOC Marines are trained to use unconventional warfare. Unconventional warfare uses sneaky, hidden techniques.

SABOTAGE

MARSOC Marines secretly destroy, disarm, or take enemy weapons. They also blow up caves or bridges the enemy uses.

GUERRILLA FIGHTING

With this technique MARSOC Marines surprise the enemy with **raids**. These quick attacks are carried out by a small unit of soldiers. The object of guerrilla fighting is to hassle enemies and wear them down until they give up.

URBAN COMBAT

One of the most dangerous places to fight is inside a city. There are many places for snipers to hide. No building can be considered safe. MARSOC soldiers learn to keep moving, stay in shadows, and not to cross open spaces.

UNCONVENTIONAL ASSISTED RECOVERY (UAR)

UAR means a MARSOC team rescues a person or group from enemy territory. Unlike a regular recovery, a UAR is done in secret, often at night.

raid—a sudden, surprise attack on a place

COUNTERTERRORISM

Terrorists are dangerous enemies. MARSOC Marines are trained to fight and defeat them. To combat terrorism, MARSOC soldiers work to:

- ➡ capture or kill terrorist leaders.
- ➡ destroy places where terrorists hide.
- ➡ destroy or disrupt terrorists' communications systems.
- ➡ prevent money or resources from getting to terrorists.
- ➡ destroy terrorist training camps.

MARSOC Marines help foreign militaries keep terrorist groups from growing in their countries. In 2010 MARSOC Marines trained troops from Senegal and Mali. U.S. leaders felt these two African nations could become hideouts for terrorists. The people of Senegal and Mali speak French. French-speaking Marines were sent in to teach their African partners **marksmanship** and urban fighting skills. This training has helped stop terrorist activity in the area.

marksmanship—skill at aiming and shooting guns

Chapter 2

A LONG HISTORY

The U.S. Marines Special Operations Regiment began in 2006. But Marine special ops are not new. The Marines have had special ops forces for many years. They just went by different names.

MARINE RAIDERS

The Marine Raiders were formed in 1942. The Raiders fought in the Far East during World War II (1939–1945). At that time, the Japanese had taken over many islands across the South Pacific. The needed soldiers who could sneak onto the islands, find out what the enemy was doing, and carry out raids.

Raiders used dogs to help them scout the land and deliver messages.

The Raiders specialized in amphibious raids. They secretly approached islands in rubber boats and sneaked ashore. Carrying submachine guns and automatic rifles, the small teams located enemy bases and airfields. They radioed this information back to Allied ships. Raiders used guerrilla-style strikes to take over hills and beaches. The Raiders were disbanded in 1944 because their missions were accomplished.

Guadalcanal, Solomon Islands [August 1942]—The Raiders led the invasion of this Japanese island. The goal was to take over an important airfield. The Raiders helped capture the island east of the airfield. This move allowed regular troops to take the entire island.

Tugali, Solomon Islands [August 1942]—The Japanese had control of this tiny island and its seaplane base. The Raiders landed on a rugged, undefended stretch of beach. They caught the Japanese soldiers there by surprise and captured the base.

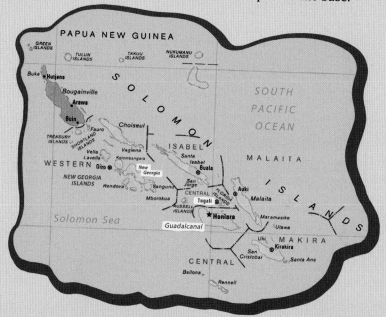

New Georgia [July 1943]—Raiders scouted out the Japanese movements on the island. They learned where enemy defenses were weakest. This information helped U.S. troops know where to invade. The U.S. invasion cut off a major supply route for the Japanese.

Fact

The Marine Raiders' rallying cry was "Gung Ho!" This saying is Chinese for "Work together!"

Allies—a group of countries that fought together in World War II, including the United States

amphibious—able to work over land and in water

FORCE RECON

In the 1950s, North Vietnam became a communist country. South Vietnam tried to be a democracy. The Vietnam War (1959–1975) erupted between the two regions. During the war the United States backed South Vietnam. By the early 1960s, American troops were sent to fight in the jungles against North Vietnam's Viet Cong army.

Ha Giang
Cao Bang
Lao Cai
Lang Son
Yen Bai
Thai Nguyen
Dien Bien
Son La
Viet Tri
Hon Gai
Hanoi ⊗
Haiphong
Hoa Binh
Nam Dinh

North Vietnam

Thanh Hoa

Vinh

The Viet Cong used guerrilla warfare. The Marines developed Force Recon units to fight this enemy. In Vietnam, Force Recon Marines had two basic missions:

deep reconnaissance—gather information about enemy size, strength, and activities

direct action—conduct short, surprise attacks and raids on the enemy

Dong Hoi

Quang Tri
Khe Sanh
Hue
Da Nang
Quang Ngai

Kon Tum
Play Cu (Pleiku)
Quy Nhon
Tuy Hoa

South Vietnam
Buon Ma Thuot
Nha Trang
Da Lat
Cam Ranh
Phan Rang-Thap Cham
Tay Ninh
Bien Hoa
Phan Thiet
Chau Doc
My Tho
Ho Chi Minh City
Long Xuyen
Can Tho
Vung Tau
Rach Gia
Soc Trang
Ca Mau
Bac Lieu

communist—a way of organizing a country so that all the land, houses, and factories belong to the government or community

The Force Recon units in Vietnam were disbanded in 1974. But Force Recon units still operate. Today Force Recon is also known as Marine Reconnaissance. This group gathers information for larger Marine forces.

Marines climb a steep bank as they head north to fight the Viet Cong.

Fact

The motto of Force Recon Marines is "Swift, Silent, Deadly."

DETACHMENT ONE

To fight in Operation Iraqi Freedom (2003–2011), the Marine Corps formed a new special operations team. This group was called Detachment One, or Det One. This unit was specially trained to fight rebels in Iraq.

The men of Det One were tough, rugged, and smart. These soldiers learned new methods of fighting in very close quarters. They used speed and shock to overcome the enemy.

Det One was disbanded in 2006. It was replaced by a new special operations force—MARSOC.

MISSION PROFILES:
Detachment One In Iraq

May 2004

Det One soldiers found and questioned two people who were thought to be helping terrorists. From them, the soldiers learned where a terrorist lived. The Det One Marines made a plan and moved fast. They headed out from the base at 1:00 a.m. With night vision goggles and Global Positioning System (GPS) units, they rode through Baghdad. At the target house, they climbed over the wall around the home. One team headed to the house. Another team went to a nearby workshop. They blasted the doors of both places open. The terrorists were quickly caught. The mission was finished by 2:00 a.m.

June 2004

Det One Marines were sent to capture a former Iraqi army officer. The officer had taken cover in a house with a wall around it. Det One Marines set explosives to blow the door open. But the charge misfired. A second blast blew the door open, but the element of surprise had been lost. Gunfire erupted. But Det One Marines were still able to capture the officer.

MARSOC

MARSOC is part of a larger group called the United States Special Operations Command (SOCOM). SOCOM decides what missions to send MARSOC soldiers on.

SOCOM

SOCOM coordinates all U.S. special operations missions.

Naval Special Warfare (NSW)

NSW includes the Navy SEALS, SEAL delivery teams, and boat units. NSW specializes in operations at sea.

United States Army Special Operations Command (USASOC)

USASOC includes the Army Rangers, airborne units, and Green Berets. These U.S. Army soldiers specialize in counterterrorism and land operations.

Air Force Special Operations Command (AFSOC)

AFSOC includes Combat Control and Pararescue. AFSOC provides air support for special ops missions.

Marine Special Operations Command (MARSOC)

MARSOC soldiers are expert land and sea special ops Marines.

A MARSOC unit has 14 men. Each unit has one captain and one radio operator. The other 12 men are divided into three teams. The teams can work separately or all together.

The captain is in charge of the mission.

The radio operator handles communication between the teams and air and ground support.

Each team has a leader who is in charge of riflemen.

Each team has an automatic rifleman, an assistant automatic rifleman, and a rifleman. The riflemen fight the enemy and defend the team.

Chapter 3

WHAT IT TAKES

The tryout process for MARSOC is extremely difficult. To be considered, a Marine must have served for at least 2 years. The Marine's physical and mental test scores must be high enough. And he can't have disciplinary action on his record.

If a Marine is eligible to try out, he attends Assessment and Selection (A&S). This course is held five or six times a year and lasts 19 days. In A&S Marines must prove they can meet the challenges of being a special operator.

To pass A&S a Marine must:

hike 12 miles (19 kilometers) with a load of 45 pounds (20 kg) in four hours.

pass the MARSOC swim test. In full uniform without boots, a soldier must tread water for 15 minutes. Then he must swim 984 feet (300 meters).

pass a background check. This check determines if a Marine can be trusted with secret information.

pass the physical exam. This exam includes blood tests, heart and brain exams, and X-rays. The soldier must even have his teeth checked.

pass intelligence testing and a mental evaluation.

During A&S the Marines learn stretching exercises that help them through the tough physical training.

Fact

Fewer than 50 percent of those who try A&S are allowed to move on to special ops training.

BECOMING A MARSOC MARINE

Enter Phase 1

PHYSICAL FITNESS
Prove you're physically fit by completing running, weight-lifting, and agility exercises.

HAND-TO-HAND COMBAT
Learn, practice, and demonstrate excellent martial arts skills.

URBAN AND RURAL RECONNAISSANCE
Learn and demonstrate how to get secret information in cities and in the country.

PHOTO AND INFO COLLECTING
Learn to take photos and gather information behind enemy lines.

Enter Phase 3

RIFLE AND PISTOL MARKSMANSHIP
Learn to shoot different types of weapons with accuracy.

RURAL AND URBAN RAIDS
Practice attacking a target in a city and a country setting.

Marines who pass A&S move on to the Marine Special Operations School. They must pass this difficult schooling in order to be called MARSOC Marines. See what you're up against if you want to be a MARSOC Marine.

AMPHIBIOUS TRAINING

You must scuba dive, operate small boats, and fire weapons at sea.

SERE (SURVIVAL, EVASION, RESISTANCE, ESCAPE)

Survive in a jungle for five days with only a knife. You will be captured and put in prison. You then must escape.

Enter Phase 2
SCOUT SWIMMING OPERATIONS

Jump from a helicopter into the ocean. Swim to shore and check out a landing beach. Then signal to the main force to come ashore.

DEMOLITION

Practice and demonstrate proper use of explosives.

Enter Phase 4

OPERATION DERNA BRIDGE

Use all the skills learned in previous training in a "war game." You will train, advise, and fight with a fake foreign army. You will face attacks and perform rescues and escapes.

Welcome to MARSOC!

27

Chapter 4

GEAR, WEAPONS, AND VEHICLES

MARSOC's equipment varies from mission to mission. But the basic gear usually includes the following:

Helmet—The Future Assault Shell Technology (FAST) helmet is lightweight. But it still offers good protection from blasts. Night vision goggles can be put on the helmet to allow Marines to see at night.

Goggles—Oakley Radar goggles have flat black frames and non-reflective lenses. The lenses don't reflect sunlight that could attract unwanted attention.

MHRS—The Mission Helmet Recorder System (MHRS) has an LED light and a video/audio recorder. It also has a digital camera with a lens the size of a pencil eraser.

Uniform—The lightweight shirt and pants are flame resistant. The gloves are flame and heat resistant.

Hydration Backpack—This backpack holds 3 quarts (3 liters) of water with room for food and supplies.

Body Armor—A soft vest hooks at the shoulders and waist to protect the body from gunfire. It weighs about 30 pounds (14 kg).

Boots—Assault boots have inner shock absorbers and rubber soles for traction.

WEAPONS

MARSOC Marines choose the best weapons for each mission. These are some of their go-to weapons.

STRIDER SMF FRAME LOCK FOLDING KNIFE

This multi-use weapon is used for close-quarters combat. It's also useful for digging or scraping.

KIMBER CUSTOM

This semi-automatic pistol weighs 38 ounces (1 kg) and is fitted with a 7- or 8-round magazine. It's used in close-quarters combat.

M136 AT4 ROCKET LAUNCHER

The M136 is a 15-pound (7-kg) shoulder-held weapon. It can send an explosive hurling toward a target at 950 feet (290 m) per second.

M-4 CARBINE

This gas-operated, magazine-fed gun is fired from the shoulder. It can fire as a semi automatic or in three-round bursts.

M249 SQUAD AUTOMATIC WEAPON

The M249 is a light machine gun. It can fire 750 to 1,000 rounds per minute.

SPECIAL OPERATIONS COMBAT RIFLE (SCAR)

This assault rifle can hit a target up to 655 yards (600 m) away. It fires 625 rounds per minute.

MP5 9 MM SUBMACHINE GUN

The MP5 is extremely accurate and can fire 700 to 900 rounds per minute. It weighs less than 8 pounds (4 kg).

AIR TRAVEL

One of MARSOC's most important jobs is patrolling. Usually patrolling is done on foot. But sometimes the enemy is far from a MARSOC base. For those missions, Marines are flown in on helicopters. They slide down ropes to the target area.

The **MV-22 OSPREY TILTROTOR** is one aircraft that brings MARSOC Marines to missions. The Tiltrotor is unique because it is a helicopter when it flies vertically. But it's an airplane when the rotors are down. The Tiltrotor can go as fast and as far as an airplane. But it can take-off and hover like a helicopter.

The **UH-1Y VENOM** is a small but useful helicopter. Rockets and machine guns are mounted on the Venom. Gunners can fire on a target from the air. MARSOC uses the Venom to carry Marines, provide fire cover, and fly wounded soldiers to safety.

The **CH-46 SEA KNIGHT** is one of the most-used military helicopters. It can carry up to 17 fully-loaded Marines or up to 4,000 pounds (1,814 kg) of supplies on a sling.

LAND AND SEA TRAVEL

MARSOC missions are carried out on land and sea. For these missions, MARSOC soldiers have some powerful vehicles to get them where they need to go.

GROUND MOBILITY VEHICLE (GMV-M)

The GMV-M can tackle the most rugged land. It can cut through 30 inches (76 centimeters) of water.

The GMV-M can transport a four-man crew 275 miles (443 km) on one tank of fuel.

This vehicle has four-wheel drive. It also has a V-8 turbo-charged engine for plenty of power.

The GMV-M is armored and carries armored machine guns. Soldiers are protected from blasts while still being able to fire on the enemy.

INTERIM FAST ATTACK VEHICLE [IFAV]

The IFAV is a lightweight truck. It is equipped with weapons, such as machine guns and grenade launchers. The IFAV has a top speed of 96 miles (154 km) per hour.

LAV-25

The LAV-25 is truly amphibious. It only takes three minutes to change it from a land vehicle to a sea-going vessel.

HMMWV [HUMVEE]

The Humvee can carry troops, guns, and missile launchers. This vehicle can also be used as an ambulance. The HMMWV has four-wheel drive and operates well on very rough land.

Chapter 5

THE MISSIONS

MARSOC Marines play a huge role in the war against terror. MARSOC Marines arrived in Afghanistan in 2007. Their mission was to clear the Taliban from Helmand Province. This was a dangerous mission. The Taliban protected that area fiercely because poppies grew there. Poppies produce opium, an illegal drug. The Taliban sold the drug to pay for weapons and other war supplies.

AFGHANISTAN

Kabul

Helmand Province

MARSOC Marines moved in to clear out a group of Taliban fighters. At the edge of a village, the Taliban began firing at them from the top of a hill. Mortar fire and rocket-propelled grenades rained down on them. The Marines could not reach the Taliban on foot. So they used their vehicles loaded with .50 caliber machine guns and grenade launchers. Then aircraft screamed overhead, bombing the Taliban. The Taliban's control of the area was destroyed.

Special ops soldiers and Afghan police worked together to stop the Taliban.

Taliban—a political group in Afghanistan that uses terror to spread its ideas

DAILY

FIREFIGHT!

Nov. 6, 2009

(Bala Murghab, a village in Badghis Province, Afghanistan)

MARSOC Marines were sent to recover the bodies of two soldiers who had drowned in Badghis Province. Army Special Forces and Afghan army soldiers joined the Marines.

Just as the unit entered the village, the Taliban attacked. The Marines took cover and shot back. Hospital corpsman Amilcar Rodriguez was traveling with the MARSOC Marines. As the battle raged, he climbed to a rooftop. Rodriguez spotted Taliban snipers aiming at a Marine and two Afghan soldiers. He fired 200 rounds from his M249 machine gun, killing the snipers.

Suddenly Rodriguez was hit in the chest and arm. A MARSOC Marine climbed to the rooftop. He pulled Rodriguez to safety. The original mission was later carried out successfully.

NEWS

Rodriguez receives the
Silver Star for his actions.

|||||||| |||||| ||||| |||||||| |||||| |||||||||

BATTLE IN FARAH PROVINCE

Date: June 2008
Place: Farah Province, western Afghanistan

Another Marine takes over the grenade launcher, but he's also shot.

7

The second vehicle moves forward, keeping up fire. A shot hits the Marine running the grenade launcher.

6

Another team of Marine vehicles comes to provide support. A hospital corpsman leaves one of these vehicles and runs through the firefight to the second vehicle.

8

9

The hospital corpsman is unable to give first aid because of the rapid enemy fire. He uses an M203 grenade launcher to shoot grenades up toward the enemy. The Taliban bullets stop.

1 MARSOC Marines in three vehicles drive into a narrow canyon. Rocky cliffs surround them on both sides.

2 The men in the lead vehicle spot several caves and two cars blocking them.

3 They check the cars to make sure they're not rigged with bombs. They're clean.

4 Taliban fighters open fire from the top of a ridge. Four or five Marines are hit. All Marines begin firing up toward the enemy.

5 In the second vehicle, one Marine fires the M240G machine gun while another fires an automatic grenade launcher.

10 The firefight continues until air support zooms in. Air support destroys the Taliban stronghold. One Marine dies from the injuries he received during the attack.

WORKING TOWARD PEACE

MARSOC missions are often focused on bringing peace to an area. Soldiers do this by driving out enemies and helping people rebuild. Many MARSOC peace missions have been in Afghanistan.

The Taliban controlled the Darrah-I-Bum district in Afghanistan. But in 2010 the Afghan army arrived along with MARSOC Marines and other special operations teams. These combined forces hit the Taliban with grenades and small-arms fire. The fight pushed the Taliban out.

In 2009 MARSOC Marines provided security in Herat Province, Afghanistan. With MARSOC Marines keeping the enemy away, a medical team was able to see up to 350 patients each Thursday. With the help of MARSOC Marines, a major health clinic in Nawa reopened along with several schools.

MARSOC Marines talk with local people to build trust.

Women Helping Women

Even though women can't be members of MARSOC, some female Marines have become part of special ops teams. In Afghanistan, their role is to work with Afghan women. According to tradition, Afghan women can't talk to men outside their family. Female Marines help build trust. They pass out aspirin and vitamins and help at clinics. They are also fully equipped and trained to fight if necessary.

NOW AND IN THE FUTURE

MARSOC Marines need the best equipment to get their missions done. Future special ops gear is a highly guarded secret. But advances in technology give some clues as to what's coming.

MARSOC Marines may someday wear helmets with voice-activated drop-down screens. On the screens they'll be able to see where enemy soldiers are hiding.

The uniform of the future might have in-fabric air conditioning. It might also have sensors to monitor a soldier's health. The uniforms will probably also be sprayed with liquid armor. This substance remains soft until it's hit with a bullet. It then becomes as hard as steel.

Warfare has changed. Armies and navies no longer clash in great battles. Terrorists are the largest threat to peace today. Special operations forces like MARSOC combat these enemies today and will continue to do so in the future. These Marines will do whatever it takes to defend the United States of America.

GLOSSARY

Allies (AL-eyz)—a group of countries that fought together in World War II; some of the Allies were the United States, Canada, Great Britain, and France

amphibious (am-FI-bee-uhs)—able to work over land and in water

civilian (si-VIL-yuhn)—a person who is not in the military

communist (KAHM-yuh-nist)—a way of organizing a country so that all the land, houses, and factories belong to the government or community

compound (KAHM-pownd)—a grouping of separate homes often enclosed by a fence or wall

marksmanship (MARKS-muhn-ship)—skill at aiming and shooting guns

raid (RAYD)—a sudden, surprise attack on a place

reconnaissance (ree-KAH-nuh-suhnss)—a mission to gather information about an enemy

Taliban (TAHL-i-bahn)—a political group in Afghanistan that uses terror to spread its ideas

terrorist (TER-uhr-ist)—a person who uses violence to kill or injure to make people and governments afraid

READ MORE

Goldish, Meish. *Marine Corps: Civilian to Marine.* Becoming a Soldier. New York: Bearport, Pub., 2011.

Loria, Laura. *Marine Force Recon.* U.S. Special Forces. New York: Gareth Stevens Pub., 2012.

Portman, Michael. *Marine Corps.* U.S. Military Forces. New York: Gareth Stevens, 2011.

INTERNET SITES

FactHound offers a safe, fun way to find Internet sites related to this book. All of the sites on FactHound have been researched by our staff.

Here's all you do:

Visit www.facthound.com

Type in this code: 9781429686587

INDEX